Y0-BLS-704

Comments on Madeline Tiger's earlier work:

"To read Madeline Tiger's poetry is like flowing with the river of life itself. Quickly, slowly around bends and curves, dashed over stones, full of human traffic. Life, love and death are her subjects—not the abstractions but the details, and she gets the details right."
—*Alicia Ostriker*

"These are poems I want to carry around and read to friends at crisis moments in their lives... as beautiful as they are on paper, they are musical in the way old fashioned rhyming poems are: they go into you and stay... Her courage to tell the truth wins our respect and confidence... These poems skirt the pitfalls of autobiographical writing because of their profound nakedness, their unsparing look at the speaker, and because of their lucidity in form, emotion, and idea..."
—*Toi Derricotte*

"I much admire Madeline Tiger's poetry of observation, her keen memory and her holding of things dear... I also admire her poems of pure imagination, dreamy and scary... I look at these poems of thirty years and realize what a strong poet she is. Most of all I realize her extraordinary courage in the face of unbearable loss."
—*Gerald Stern*

"Having sailed the seas of love and loss, Madeline Tiger finds terra firma in the word, in the poem. Here is the result: 30 years of courage and craft, passion and precision, in a rock solid addition to the contemporary canon." —*Paul Genega*

"In *The Atheist's Prayer* Madeline Tiger never forgets, even in the most intimate moments, that "truth is ...like the old inveterate river that holds clouds." Tiger encompasses, with a tender embrace, a life made whole; her ministrations do not deny its sorrows, and she is glad to celebrate its hard-won triumphs... It is the caring in these quietly intelligent poems which makes living in this world possible."
—*Burt Kimmelman*

FROM THE VIEWING STAND

Madeline Tiger

DOS MADRES
2011

DOS MADRES PRESS INC.
P.O.Box 294, Loveland, Ohio 45140
www.dosmadres.com   editor@dosmadres.com

Dos Madres is dedicated to the belief that the small press is essential to the vitality of contemporary literature as a carrier of the new voice, as well as the older, sometimes forgotten voices of the past. And in an ever more virtual world, to the creation of fine books pleasing to the eye and hand.

Dos Madres is named in honor of Vera Murphy and Libbie Hughes, the "Dos Madres" whose contributions have made this press possible.

Dos Madres Press, Inc. is an Ohio Not For Profit Corporation and a 501 (c) (3) qualified public charity. Contributions are tax deductible.

Executive Editor: Robert J. Murphy

Illustration & Book Design: Elizabeth H. Murphy
www.illusionstudios.net

Typset in Adobe Garamond Pro & Trajan Pro

ISBN 978-1-933675-67-1

First Edition

Copyright 2011 Dos Madres Press inc.
All rights to reproduction of the text, quotation, and translation reside with the author.

ACKNOWLEDGEMENTS

The Hague Review: "Prologue"
Paterson Literary Review: "Brass Rings"
Spillway: "Iris"
Rutherford Red Wheel Barrow: "Terry Cloth"
Edison Review: "Sunday Visit"
Asbury Park Press: "Potsy"
Jewish Women's Literary Annual: "They Said Girls
    Couldn't Build Igloos"
Eddy: "Heidi Placates the Great Father"
The Mulberry Review: "The Duck Pond"
New Moon Review: "Thanksgiving Pride"
Curbside Review and *cherryblossomreview* (on-line):
    "The Weeping Cherry Tree"

Photographer for the author's portrait: Sybil Holland
Secretarial assistant: Christine Kaminski

Dedicated to
my sister Babs
and
my life long friend Meryl

TABLE OF CONTENTS

1 – Prologue
2 – Brass Rings
5 – From the Viewing Stand
8 – Iris
10 – Terry Cloth
13 – Sunday Visit
16 – Potsy
18 – They Said Girls Couldn't Build Igloos
20 – Heidi Placates the Great Father
22 – The Duck Pond
23 – Thanksgiving Pride
24 – The Weeping Cherry Tree

PROLOGUE
– sequence at a writers conference

First,
she was seduced
into her head
where she slept
with Emily
opened sentences
cracked words
and possessed
nothing.

Below,
in the deep
her body began
the ancient flow
the old red song.

Archaeologists
are busy in museums
deciphering the dark scratches
that may mean music.

BRASS RINGS

Hold hands
        at 65th Street
Cross the hexagons

It starts slowly
You hear it from under the bridge,
when the tiny accordion speeds, there is
this challenge to
you want to   let go
one hand,
        oh

Old man
old man
with your painted monsters
with your creased face
your arm cranking
fate, you offer   me
jewels.
I am falling
to disgrace.
I had a box full of silver rings then
I could look deep
into my collection. Mother
made me give the rings back
before we moved
out of the silver city.
Mother
said it was dishonest,
she said we mustn't keep
what we don't need, she said
we had no right
to the silver rings I had caught
over the small years riding

round and round. She taught me
the rules of our family.
We had everything, she said,
and other children needed to
      catch the rings.

I was quiet (or maybe crying).
Then she told me
the rings were not worth it,
not silver, "only brass,"
they would "tarnish" quickly,
(that meant turn color,
that meant get ugly, so of course
we wouldn't want them.)

And anyway, the extra baggage
would be a nuisance.

I was driven off to the suburbs
with strong morals, an
evil secret,
and the memory
of something taken.

Coda:
"Do you feel sorry for the little girl, Ma?"
says Barbara Joan, "or do you feel sorry for yourself?"
She had seen me crying, writing and crying,
so she gets me
to talk about Mother.

She wants me to
absolve my mother
and offer her

the joy of mothering,
but the floor turns faster
and her face recedes
outside the music.

FROM THE VIEWING STAND
– Woodmere Club, 1938

I am four. Nobody told me
how to climb this marquee.*
Scary heights, all those
empty benches. Sky　far
out there and the trees,
I'm almost as high as
those leafy branches.
Mommy and Daddy are far
down, they warned me
I must stay up here.
I don't want to stay
or go. I only know
how far it is between us
and how hard he swings.
Sometimes he misses but
he keeps on
swinging. Oh. And I know
she's very careful, her little
white skirt is careful, her arm
is too, slowly going back and
out and hitting, she hits
very carefully, she watches that
little ball, she doesn't look anywhere
else, not up here, not at Daddy,
(and whatever she's smiling at
in the air, I never saw her so
happy except in the mirror
when she's getting dressed
and I'm hiding behind her bed
to watch her put on the blue gown
and those tiny pearls.)

Only once, I think, she looked at
Mr. Cozzoloo, when he moved
to the white line near her (I tried
to hear what he said, I think he said
nice.) She only looks at the net
while she goes around to the other
side after a long time. That's when
they shout *set*, and Daddy gets even
more serious. He rushes to the back of
his court and stands there hunched over
his racquet, bending his knees up and down,
one knee, then the other one, over and over
like marching but not moving. He's ready.

Then, before it all starts up again with
the ball, she turns her head and squints
and looks up at the marquee and waves,
as if I'm a grown-up on a train
and she's doing the fare-well part of
a story again. But Daddy frowns,
he hits his racquet on the ground.
He wants her to pay attention. Is that
her job? Mr. Cozzoloo has a big wrist-
watch he watches. Why am I the one
going away? It's summer. Soon I'll be
old enough to go in "the deep" of the sound
where the dock has dangerous barnacles
and it's so dark way down nobody can
touch bottom. But I'll be brave,
I'll be out of the "crib" by the sandbox
where the little kids kick and pretend
they're swimming. I won't wear a life-
preserver or a cap either, and I'll float
whenever I get tired of moving
my arms and legs. I'll know how good it feels

to be all alone in the sun in the deep cold.
Mommy says I can go away to day-camp soon,
and then, when I'm ten, to sleep-away camp.
They say they're teaching me things, they even
ask if I want to come down closer, sometime,
and have a proper tennis lesson. I say yes,
but I know the secret of being in this
family already— in our house, and at this club.
Look how good I am at climbing
the highest white railings all by myself.

* *"Marquee" was the word used for the viewing stand.*

IRIS

The iris were taller than
I –in my sundress–
the purple in tough rows.

I remember the odorous
air there, the heavy prose
of intoxicant fearfulness

and sweeter than those
peeling bent petals purpling
high air, there was

the sense of extent, a surging
of how they went on in vastness.
Maybe I was watching them flow

a few spaces from the bottom step
of the long white porch. They sent
back their fragrance, enveloping

me and the white pillars,
the white door, house, windows,
all that empty and unfamiliar

dwelling where I was
placed, standing, on the veranda,
where I peed, cried silently, froze.

Sin, the sweet smell, does
tricks on a child's
frail body. Nobody knows

what I thought— releasing
pee on top of the afternoon stasis
of iris, mansion, sky, freezing

image. After cold years
of re-call, I practice the scene—
with perfume like ether. I sink in

gorgeously as beauty comes
from the thick surge of light, massed
iris. Their dense odor lifts me, I know this.

I don't know where my parents
were— mother in jodhpurs, father
smiling, just along for her excursion—

or what went wrong
when they returned, ashamed
to find the wet child on

the veranda. Pause. Her name
caw cawed. Clatter of reprimands
behind the hooves. I don't remember

how I couldn't hear or
how I rose above piss-
wet panties wet socks

and a wet party dress,
how I kept the irises benign
in their listing, heavily

gathered, how I dragged them,
that sweetness, enfolding me
through the hollow of history.

TERRY CLOTH
– for my mother who married a Lang, Hewlett, NY, 1943

I only remember the towel
and not the touch
of towels or Mother's hands.
Heavy white towels, thick and hot
in the crowded room with a Swastika
I sketched in the steamy window
with my index finger. Fear
furrowing the air, the towels
supposed to soothe me, Mother
supposed to protect me, so shy
so blind-sighted she couldn't see
the sign, or the monsters coming
with crosses and claws. The flames
I saw. And in my eyes
the dark line of Langs, the Debrecen
Langs descended from Bodony hay-farms,
set out on Austrian paths, on Dutch and
Italian and English paths, to Argentinian paths
across the ocean of loss, here. Fear doesn't allow
erasure with towel-drying
or the long forgetting my mother learned
in her lean orphan American years, safe years,
university years, her stripped blank years and kept
in her hushed married years. Fear
deepens and singes and blinds, and the safety
of the warm after-bath air silently fills
with stories of farms and journeys and names
we never name, the eastern music we never
hear, the cut lines, the short breaths, the
untranslated undone unspoken unsung songs
my grandmother sang, and the sacred secrets
Mother doesn't know. How can she
tell me acres I can't ask? How can she

say the half she accepted, married,
the horrible story, that history of
unburied truth
she almost
didn't herself
know, the
one word
I work
to make
more clear
on the dark
on the glass
the question
I –if not, who else– have
to bear. A terry-cloth
towel from Macy's can't dry
the invisible tears. Why
was who was where they/we
and below the word
the sign and behind
the sign the deed
and in the deed
the farm and
on the farm
family and
of the family
history
gone
language
gone
song
gone
Granny's brothers sisters hay-cart cousins country village
of Langs
gone. How could Mother know the words

to say to a child and why
would she try
to tell a child. Even so
why do they always say
*dry dry, dry, don't cry,
get dry.*

SUNDAY VISIT

Jovial Uncle Eph, that old man
gnarling toward the end of the garden,
gnashing. "Jovial" the grown-ups call him.
They're having tea on the porch. Do they
see? Is this the game? Is he a gnome?

His pince nez is slipping, and what's that
cane doing up? Uh oh, his heavy shoes
are coming clump clump. Look, he's
out of breath making that effort at
galloping down the grass, the yard
a sudden jumble, his laugh does not
sound kind, it's more like a snort,

but we've been assured he's
a nice uncle, he's only trying
to be friendly. Now we're running
in a straight line to the hedgerow.
Now, cornered, we go flying
back at an angle, behind the swing set,
he's coming quicker, the chuckle a
breathy *heh heh*, and he's close,
urging *tickle tickle*, and my gut
seizes up
with can't
can't move, can't stop.
Frozen– gotta run keeps me going.
Babsy follows, laughing hard

so hard her voice might knock her over
and we'd be done for. Uncle Eph close
and faster after us, we're tripping
around the swings and apple trees where
last week I was Snow White and

she was all the dwarfs and the witch was
the prince was— now I can't remember, now

the cane crook reaches me and hooks
cold, hard around my neck, and he's
huge behind it, pulling me toward
his belly, pushing and pulling my

head, my head a yo-yo not spinning, jutting
back and forth— toward, away, stiff.
I see the buttons on his vest, my throat is
closing tight, I can't call, I can't say stop,
the long shiny stick jerks again, I mustn't take
my next step. Has he won? Has he

won? His *heh heh heh* goes over
the lawn and... Do "they" hear the *ho ho*?
The cane loosens, it lets me go. My sister is free,
we fall to the grass, Babsy and me, both of us,
a shambles. The grown-ups are still

there, on the porch. How many? Four, five?
Now he's limping up the steps. Tea time
a tinkly echo, shadow forms moving
behind the screen door: Daddy, Mother,
aunts, uncles, they wave a little, waving us in,

crooking fingers, maybe they're smiling,
they're still talking, they keep talking
soft and low in that distance.
One likes lemon slices with his tea, one
likes big sugar lumps. Daddy will demand brandy.
Mother will get it and pour it and sit
and cross her legs and hold up her cup and sip her tea.

We will go in and hear Aunt Millie sigh and
let Uncle Reuben's old tobacco-smelly moustache
scratch against our cheeks, we'll try not to breathe.
Then we'll cross the slate floor and sit on the glider
close to each other and make one vanilla wafer each
last a long time. We won't look in the corner
where Uncle Eph is plumped in the wicker chair
breathing hard, going *mm-mm* before he slurps his tea,
the cup rattling against the saucer,
the handle of his cane hooked over his knee.

POTSY

In Hewlett the "back door"
led from the side of
the brick house down steps
to a little "sidewalk"

(the only "sidewalk" in
the neighborhood)
where we drew
potsy squares and hopped

over the lines for years
chalking them up again
whenever they faded.
We threw our stones

into the numbers, forever
bending one foot in the air.
Over the summers
sweet alyssum cropped up

("madwort") along the borders
with ageratum behind those,
purple furze balls & the white
lace, purple & white, over &

over, clumps and rows.
We kept hopping in our geo-
metrics— of chalk, cement, chalk
squares, cement blocks, chalk

squares, bounded by flowering and the brick
steps to the kitchen door.

Last year I stood there.
Two small boys' bikes were thrown
down, as if in a quarrel

on the sidewalk
where we'd had the squares.
Two sunken bins for
garbage are buried there now,

their lids have step-down
pedals for the front of a foot
to push, right where
our geometric designs had us

let fly
pebbles toward winning
infinite potsy innings.

THEY SAID GIRLS
COULDN'T BUILD IGLOOS
– after Marie Howe

but we did
one afternoon
in an ice-chunk time
and we put on the roof
ourselves, our wool hats
tighter and warmer
every minute, every minute
we worked, and we were all
girls, Meryl and me,
we wouldn't let Babsy help
much, but we let her in there
when we said come in
for the special occasion that afternoon.
And we were hungry, so
hungry that (I can't remember how)
we persuaded Mother, could it have been
pride that girls could build
such a thing or anything
impractical? and so strong while it stood?
She was never proud of us,
never before or after
that day, but that day she,
of all people— patroness of rules
and regulator of meals, parser-out of
afternoon snacks, she
from in the big brick house, in the back
somewhere, not the kitchen, maybe
the sun parlor, it must have been a bleak day,
maybe from upstairs— from her chaise lounge
(to the left at the top of the stairs,
the spindles and balustrades so still and cool
like the lines between don't and do) she

for that one time broke the rules, and somehow
there, in our warm snug igloo that we had just
built ourselves, were —on a small plate from the pantry—
Oreos (she always called them Hydrox, but we said Oreos) oh,
we were so content, smug, we even dared
to break them apart one by one by one (there were probably
six), this was never allowed, and scrape the white icing slowly off
with our front teeth and lick it up. Our eyes must have been
glowing in the dark hollow, we barely spoke, we knew what we
were like, we were Eskimos. Even Babsy, she kept appropriately
still, in awe of performance. Then our father came home
with his briefcase and his fedora and his worried look
                                             and he looked,
and maybe he was dumbstruck and maybe not,
                                                  we never knew.
He stood there a little while while we huddled inside
and looked through our ice-door where we'd set the chunks
                                           in an arch
                                                 to hold over
and we looked up at him
               standing there, very tall,
                   his dark winter coat over his business suit.
Then he stepped across the kitchen path into the house, and soon
there was a chill in the air and that long afternoon was over
and we were ready to squirm out and say good-bye, Meryl and I,
and she went home and I must have gone up to my room.
I know this, not from a story they ever told
but by heart
because that day
is walled in a sweet casing
apart from the brick house and all the large stucco rooms.
Sweet as ice, huge chunks
sweet as heavy breath, sweet as Oreo cream
sweet as wool caps with wool braids
and sweet as work, as sweat, as girls in a huddle,
nobody else in the world could ever come in there.

HEIDI PLACATES THE GREAT FATHER
– for Aimée Rhum, after seeing "The Sorrow and the Pity"

(singing) "We'll
always come back to Sev'rance,
for Sev'rance is HOME SWEET HOME . . ."

Summer
in the Adirondack air
and Santa Claus
came across Paradox Lake.

We painted a sign of 10 ducks
and named our cabin "Ackie's Quacks".

I swallowed a button when I saw a snake
and had to move my bowels in the nurse's office.

We wore Navy-blue shorts, fit to last,
big saddle shoes, and braids. "Alllll-
though we may wander in lands a--parrrt,
the dream of Bunga-loo-loo is still in our hearts . . . "

It was '45 and I was 10.

The Jewish children from all over France
were rounded up and brought to Paris.
The social workers had trouble:
the children cried
and crapped in their pants,
and Laval said they must be sent off,
so they were sent to Buchenwald.
We were playing a boring game of
volley ball
when the news came: Hip! Hip!
Hooray! The War half ended!

I found out 40 years later
it wasn't even V-J Day:
It was August 8th, the
Big–A Day.

That summer I was Heidi
in the camp play:
Heidi on the mountain, eating cheese,
Heidi meeting Peter among the goats,
Heidi in the cottage, placating the Great Father.

I felt the part
and was so authentic
that the Seniors wept.

THE DUCK POND
– *South Orange, 1949*

Blades slice air, slide
hot over the ice. I feel
the flush rise to my face.
Scarves fly.
Birds crossing Cameron Field
escape further south.
I am riding
currents, dying for love.

My father waits in the car.
I pray he won't get out.
Night falls. Someone passes
without seeing me. His face
mortifies. The future
is blank, the sky
full of stars
I don't notice.

THANKSGIVING PRIDE

I felt proud finally
making new friends
in college, Christian girls,
as my father had said I should.
I was proud coming home at Thanksgiving.
I hollered through the door and up the center hall
in the great glee of crossing lines, head high.
My father asked many questions
from the end of the dinner table.
Then his face was dark,
darkness inundating pride,
a tidal wave full of ancient seaweed and star-
fish shaping themselves like iron crosses criss-
crossed the dining room. Our dinner, in wild silences,
echoed a buried scream. I had forgotten
the old family habit of lying and the power
of forbidden dreams.

THE WEEPING CHERRY TREE

Go home
to the weeping
cerisier— the blossoms,
full in Maytime, now
fallen, gave way through
slow leafing and sweep
of thin old branches.

Mud banks released
tall weeds, such savage
edges for wandering
foragers. Canada Geese
arrive wild for something
to eat in the grasses.
An ominous dark
tide seeps through
while the geese pick
field stubble and honk
en route south
in a dark formation.

Earth hardens,
air thins, greys.
Wait: some day
the cherry tree will
weep green and
burst into a rush
of infinite pink
cascading
to the ground
where the wild year
has been hiding.

MADELINE TIGER'S recent collections are *Birds of Sorrow and Joy: New and Selected Poems*, 1970-2000 (2003), *The Earth Which Is All* (2008), and *The Atheist's Prayer* (2010). Her work appears regularly in journals and anthologies. She has been teaching in state programs and private workshops since 1973 and has been a "Dodge Poet" since 1986. She has five children and seven grandchildren and lives in Bloomfield, NJ under a weeping cherry tree.

Other Books from Dos Madres Press

Michael Autrey - *From The Genre Of Silence* (2008)
Paul Bray - *Things Past and Things to Come* (2006), *Terrible Woods* (2008)
Jon Curley - *New Shadows* (2009)
Deborah Diemont - *The Wanderer* (2009)
Joseph Donahue - *The Copper Scroll* (2007)
Annie Finch - *Home Birth* (2004)
Norman Finkelstein - *An Assembly* (2004), *Scribe* (2009)
Gerry Grubbs - *Still Life* (2005), *Girls in Bright Dresses Dancing* (2010)
Richard Hague - *Burst, Poems Quickly* (2004)
Pauletta Hansel - *First Person* (2007), *What I Did There* (2011)
Michael Heller - *A Look at the Door with the Hinges Off* (2006),
    Earth and Cave (2006)
Michael Henson - *The Tao of Longing & The Body Geographic* (2010)
Eric Hoffman - *Life At Braintree* (2008), *The American Eye* (2011)
James Hogan - *Rue St. Jacques* (2005)
Keith Holyoak - *My Minotaur* (2010)
David M. Katz - *Claims of Home* (2011)
Burt Kimmelman - *There Are Words* (2007), *The Way We Live* (2011)
Richard Luftig - *Off The Map* (2006)
J. Morris - *The Musician, Approaching Sleep* (2006)
Robert Murphy - *Not For You Alone* (2004), *Life in the Ordovician* (2007)
Peter O'Leary - *A Mystical Theology of the Limbic Fissure* (2005)
Bea Opengart - *In The Land* (2011)
David A. Petreman - *Candlelight in Quintero - bilingual edition* (2011)
Paul Pines - *Reflections in a Smoking Mirror* (2011)
David Schloss - *Behind the Eyes* (2005)
William Schickel - *What A Woman* (2007)
Murray Shugars - *Songs My Mother Never Taught Me* (2011)
Nathan Swartzendruber - *Opaque Projectionist* (2009)
Jean Syed - *Sonnets* (2009)
Madeline Tiger - *The Atheist's Prayer* (2010), *From The Viewing Stand* (2011)
James Tolan - *Red Walls* (2011)
Henry Weinfield - *The Tears of the Muses* (2005),
    Without Mythologies (2008), *A Wandering Aramaean* (2012)
Donald Wellman - *A North Atlantic Wall* (2010)
Tyrone Williams - *Futures, Elections* (2004), *Adventures of Pi* (2011)
Martin Willitts Jr. - *Secrets No One Must Tell* (2011)

www.dosmadres.com